MUSINGS OF LIFE

INSHA MUKHTAR WANI

Contents

Contents

Preface

This book is a collection of poems on various themes. It's usually said that we write as per our mood so here I can say that my mood is involved in penning down these poems but at the same time I have tried to give the hues of different themes in each of them. Writing has been my passion since childhood and I used to write stories, quotes and poems on my teachers, friends and different other things that I knew about at that age. With time this passion grew and I started to write on major issues and themes. After mastering the English Literature the love of writing grew more and by the grace of Almighty I got a precious chance to publish my poetry book which is now Alhamdullilah available in market by the name " The Ink Of My Imagination". This is now the second collection of poetry which includes themes like : WOMEN EMPOWERMENT, SEASONS, LOVE, INNOCENCE,FESTIVITIES, PIOUSNESS and much more. I hope that the readers would love each theme with all their hearts.

Acknowledgements

My gratitude to Allah SWT as without His Grace and Mercy nothing would have been possible. Then my first debt is to Mr Saraf Bhat who with his sympathetic guidance helped me to publish this book. I am eternally grateful to my parents for their utmost support and some special people who played their parts in getting me here.

1. Thy precious thoughts.

How doth I elucidate,
what thy precious thoughts are to me
the reminiscence of your closure
and thy serene warmth,
take me back to that locale,
where I unwarily glimpsed the heavens
Where we first constellated,
for that resolution of our forever
not just mere thoughts,
these are the dwellings of my joy
these memories are to my dead soul,
what nature is to Wordsworth's works
These are the riches, I furnish
So for our future,
we have precious thoughts to cherish.

2. Those prickling tears.

She tries to restrain the prickling tears
that are undoable to contain
she hoards the pain of hounded heart
to balance her crushed spirit
she sits in a dark hidden corner
to shun the scorching realities
when they say that a heart can be aching
aching like your stomach or your head
She whispers to herself:
“Hammered hearts don’t see stars
battered hearts don’t have contusion”
but they speak about their sentiments that are cheap metaphors
and if you adhere to her
she nurses the truest feelings that,
“Broken hearts are actually the ones that don’t work anymore”.

3. Persisting deep in my emotions.

Persisting deep in my emotions,
when my peace is churned like butter
your tactics stand firm as mountains
hitting the flow a stumbling block
cozening the upswings,
they take me back to my placidity
When I considered you as a cavalier to my emotions,
the splash cleansed the crud and bestowed you as a scion of my fervency
here I am now with this tranquility and
the darkness of my mind is gone
the sun of realities is shining bright and
my redeemer I have found
the upheaval cleared the road to new and better days
for I settled with thy reasonableness
countering them with my fantasies.

4. Festivities.

Far from the earth,up in the heavenly sky
surrounded by the glittering stars
the moon is sighted heralding the coming of EID
the glad tidings of the season remind us of His greatness
dawning with the prayers in my country,the festivities have begun
The two days of cheeriness bring the hugs of warmth, fancy attires and tasty desserts
the love is enveloping and the children are grooming
the aroma of festival and the ambience of holiness
the souls are blessed and the bodies are dancing
espying this merriment has something beyond measure
this is the festival of love and sanctity in its treasure.

5. Women

Diadems in her heart
coronets in her soul
she is the beauty itself
she is the universe in herself
let her strength exhilarate
let her voice be heard
she is the dominion , adhere to her
she is the best opinion , cherrypick her
let her love and you will conquer
let her love and grow your demenour
she is the battle of hundred long stories
she is the castle of rubies and diamonds
the fairy of every fairytale
she is the music of nightingale
rising from every slumber,
she can turn your fire into ashes
but if you be her darling and
love her,
she will recover you from your own crashes.

6. Ink and Words

Ready to begin her poem,
she puts ink in the pen
the ink is amalgamated with emotions
and the rainbow of her heart is down on a white paper
When she writes on her nation,
the ink dries up
as true stories never get true colors
When she spills the red hue,
the words ooze blood from aged wounds
Then preferring the green and blue,
she turns into a scholar of Wordsworth
Trying on the pastel shades,
she shares her sober nature
Arduous to accomplish the theme,
she cherrypicks the white shade
Oh! How doth one can write with white on white
then she leaves it blank with still a verse
appealing for peace.

7. Unadulterated feelings

Espying you again,
hearkened me back to pristine memories
when your virginal glimpse,
sparked those unadulterated feelings
moonstruck thoughts they were
whirlwinding my mind
that lovely gaze of my reverence,
reached deep into my soul
and that heavenly bliss of your warmth
conjured deeply my senses
such was the collision of your innocence,
you got an abode in my heart
your voice has that soulful rhythm ,
that still beats in my core
when closer to you,
I breathed the air
I sensed the incense of love
and then with your single beat,
I inhaled the musk of heavens
Oh! How doth I unriddle this
as these unadulterated feelings ,
dwell in my heart

as that heavenly repose of angels.

8. My heart craves for more

My heart craves for more but
Do I deserve else?
My soul wants to fly but
Do I deserve wings?
hoards of questions bursting out
hoards of mysteries unsolved
Do I really offer myself to the best?
Do I really stand where supposed to be?
When encountered with these realities
throbs my heart in panic
blows my mind in horror
Is my outer charm of blessedness or a disguise of mysteriousness?

9. To my dearest Muzzafar Sir

To my dearest Muzzafar Sir,
Perplexed by their variable concepts
when I was left as a lonely mess
recreant lecturers with vague lectures,
when threw my mind in darkest dinges
you came as a torchbearer and
left no doubt unclear
When it was just a subject,
you made me fell in love with literature
Befuddling when I was it with just poetry,
you taught me how incredibly profound it was
You are the one I often confused with the great Shakespeare
Oh! How can one teach" Hamlet" with intimate details so rare
Here I have dairies full of your precious words
they no less than are amulets guarding my sanity with swords
I can never utter to you words like "thankyou" for,
they may belittle your dedication
You have taught me the lessons for life
acting on them can may be a petty compensation
If possible ever, I can actually write
I will try to write you

My dearest teacher, if I know a little of English Literature
I owe it all to you.
Paper, paper
I pour down and you absorb my pain
enduring all my sufferings, you ooze out the ink of relief
the ink that shines from the beams out of my soul
the ink that burnishes the words hidden deep in my nucleus
Oh! piece of paper, I tell you more than I tell people
When no human abides my throes,
being lifeless you furnish life to me'
I wonder what a piece of magic you are!
as promptly you vanish my torments
This commutation of pain and pleasure,
won't terminate until my quietus
as you being reticent to my secrets ,
will ever receive more and more treasure.

10. The Butterflies

The butterflies your voice gave me,
meander around coldly
for their life they beg,
for my colors I beseech
This hushed soul dwelling in me,
had once an abode in you
for its peace it pleads
for my conscience I appeal
Hold me back my belongings
for then,
the haze of my aura,
will fade away
as you are the mist,
to wash this crud away.

11. Your presence.

Your presence throbs my heart and
absence pinches my soul
Your glimpse blows my mind and
voice touches my core
That musk of heavens you spread on your smile and
warmth of magic for my body so fragile
Life becomes that aura of springs as I whirl in your thoughts
angels repose on my besides as I twirl in your feels
Oh! How doth I explain ,
for sure you are the reason of this happiness
Oh! Indeed ,
you are the sole savior of my blessedness.

12. Seasons of my being.

Akin to the warm afternoons,
you offer that coziness to my soul
after that scorching summer heat
you bring back life to me
just as springs does to nature
after that dearth of winters
you are the rain of monsoons,
that blooms in my heart those flowers of love
You are that pristine breeze of dawn,
that freshens me for that sound mind
when in winter birds migrate,
your arrival is an adversary to my sorrows
Thy being closer does wonders to me
just as spring does to barren land
There are seasons for world
and you are those “four in one “ of my being.

13. The rain falls.

The rain falls and
the envelope of earth is dark
dark as the sins of man
blind as the souls of twenties
the sky cries with the sound of a starving dog
with the sound of a kashmiri boy, longing for his mother's lap
behind the bars
the trees tremble like the body of a young girl
hailing from the modern society
like the innocent deer being chased by the hungry predators
the bloodshed of humanity roars higher to the skies
the air soars to evoke the dead spirits of humans
Then,
I will call up to my Lord who is with me and up from the skies
Then,
the rain falls and washes the wounds of earth
Then,
the rain falls and blows the breeze of love on earth.

14. In the early charms.

In the early charms of sun rises,
In the fresh breezes of mornings,
In the dew drops of new starts,
I fell in love with the air you breathe
I fell in love with the chirps you hear
Deep in my heart is a strange beat
cleansing it is mine since we met
In the twinkling of far stars,
In the circling of huge planets,
In the brightness of lonely moon,
I fell in love with the lights you see
I fell in love with the sound" me and thee".

15. Hurt at heart when I sigh.

Hurt at heart when I sigh,
tears roll down with a cry
flashes of memories when pass by,
through the mind with emotions high
You appear to me and that mesmerizing smile
takes away my burden like a soothing balm
Then I feel my world besides you as
else appears so futile
Then relaxes my tempest and soul is so calm.

16. I often wonder.

I often wonder thy personality
sometimes I call out to my self
little I get to know from you
then I ask my inner depths
The very issues in thy actions
the very appeal in thy words
and riots that stage in my heart
they appeal to the very you
come and let's tie knots where,
once we broke
oh! come let's count the stars,
where once we lost.

17. Deep in that hole.

Deep in that dark hole,
hides my ever lonely soul
Far from that every charm
aloof from that serene calm
Peeping through the windows of heart,
I see someone coming and setting it free
I see someone coming and making it glee
Staged that riots once it had
tangled chains once it had
Relaxing from that every mess
relieving from every stress
Who is preceding to let it dance
Who is he with the pristine glance.

18. My soul venerates.

My soul venerates his presence
and body embraces his warmth
He is the conjurer of my senses
He is the host of my fancies
That charm of morning star his face has
and the eyes have the silence of rustic nights
My earth heaves me to his skies
My mind whirls in his thoughts
His presence has the warmth of heavens
His breath has the incense of musky pearls
My eyes glitter with his glimpse
My heart beats to his moves
He is the abode of my sheer happiness
He is the host of my blessedness.

19. Those daily brabbles.

Those daily brabbles when seem to forsake us
I write a poem with hopes to fill the voids
I write to express, the unsaid words
the words that tell you better than the things I ever utter
O, my dear attend to my poetry and see,
how I inchoate your vignettes
Oh! delve into my depths and feel how I feel you
there you will meet thyself with a novel whim
may be you meet the rendition of you that is dwelling in me
and that meeting won't be mere
as then to our commitments we will forever adhere.

20. In this transient world.

In this transient world,
let's hoard memories eternal
our lives being ephemeral
let's live moments immortal
for spring blossoms,
fade in the blazing sun
Oh! let's store the charms for
each new season
To be a bedazzling guest
arriving with gifts of joy
For each new day,
to shine the beams of warmth
our mortal bodies,
let's fill with abiding love
for our souls imperishable
to heft to the skies.

21. The gardens of my heart.

The gardens of my heart, take their share of springs from
the grandeur of your face
As your aura is a majesty which enlightens my presence
in the sheer darkness of world
The essence of your breath has that musk of heavens
in which angels take their bath
Your gaze is that first ray of dawn that lightens
the gloomy nights to new brightening starts
Your warmth is the merriment of my core and
your presence is the glitter of my eyes
My garrulous soul talks to you as you make me feel heavenly
and your thoughts don't treat me casually
I roam in heavens with you
I live in fancies with you.

22. My garrulous soul.

My garrulous soul went dumb
on hearing his voice
My blurred eyes glittered like gold
on having his glimpse
I feel his presence and feel his warmth
when breezes paas by me
I see him in that orb
sparkling far in the west stary sky
Like the chirping birds, he murmurs in my ears
Like the alluring flowers, he scents my depths
As my words flow, they describe him
As my breaths breathe, I live him.

23. Like dead leaves.

Like dead leaves of autumn,
my soul has dried up
I need your warmth
need your warmth to let it live
I need your glimpse
need your glimpse for my eyes to shine
My chaotic mind wants the repose
that blissful repose in your heart
Like that charms of springs,
I want to glow in the gardens of your thoughts
I want to breathe in you to live for us
I want you to be me, to feel both of us.

24. That primeval crud.

That primeval crud of my soul,
How doth I clean?
That ghosts in my thoughts,
How doth I escape?
as in that journey to my inner self,
I wandered through wilderness
then faded my outer charms
as I found my ugly depths
and that miopia of my aura
finally vanished
and vanished to bring me back
back from that hallucinated castle
that castle called fantasies.

25. His wrinkled smile.

His wrinkled smile,
I have seen the old man shedding hidden tears
That flowing streams,
I have seen them taking deepest sighs
That glittering orb,
I have seen the moon weeping on it's loneliness
Oh! then don't praise my aura
don't flow with my charms
for, I have wandered through my wilderness
for, I have peeped through my unrefined soul.

26. My heart calls out.

My heart calls out to you
as my soul longs for that repose
Alone in the millions,
that moon mourns my solitude
Fresh breezes of springs,
stop at my window
Alluring sceneries of rustics
take deep glances at me
mesmerizing streams,
weep on this seclusion
When will you arrive
and they will behold
and then nature will be normal
and I will settle
I will regain
regain with my soul
settle with peace.

27. When my wrath.

When my wrath could raise the silent oceans
to the appalling tempests,
Your soothing words melt my heart to that deepest feel
Then I wonder, how could a heart remain silent
and make me feel better of the best
Oh! how could your innocence endure
my silly deeds
As you pacify my birse to the blissful repose
and heft my soul to heavens
Such serenity on my rage is out of love or
you see me worthless of your immersion
whatever thy detention is,
I adore this heavenly comprehension

28. Unconsciously.

Unconsciously, you had met me as a fragment
of my momentity
dwelling in my cerebellum and roaming
in my fervency,
you were always there till we met in reality
You were in the morning breeze and in the evening stars
With the rise of morning orb,
I welcomed your novel thoughts
Staring at the moon, at night
I fancied you in my eyes
and now when the fancies have met the reality,
I serenade you in my soul.

29. In my world.

In my world, the sky is not blue and
the grass is not green
The rivers don't dance in merriment
and the ponds don't embellish the sceneries
It is my world where nothing is mine
It is my world where aches my spine
In this world emotions are mere words
and clans ain't blood
The days are less candascent
and nights are more gloomy
It is my world where roads are tenebrous
It is my world where destiny is doomed
In this world that is mine, I belong to none
In my world where I exist, I merely live.

30. Summer to winter.

When in summers we met,
till these winters where the two are us
I didn't think we would ever get
as close as we have become now
Since it started, we had dark clouds
and we had bright fancies
We often have times when we need to talk but
words merely come
We have times when we need to immerse in each other but
none knows how
When we have bitter times and we loose the sense
to communicate
When tough times get us complicated and leave us in wonder
what the other is feeling and thinking
let me tell you, I believe in us and all that we share
I believe we can get through if only we open up
When love is both wicked ang good, I would use the rearmost
side
I would make us to use the wings of love to fly across the
endless sky for that never ending bliss
I have heard them saying that love is tough and
we know we have seen it much
They also say that love survives if given time to thrive

So let's make it grow for we have seasons to come
But that summer to winter, I wrote in this poem our traverse
I hope this poem can make you see that these months made me to say,
that you mean the world and much more to me.

31. Your heart terraining acts

Your heart terraining acts
How doth I climb?
You heft my soul to heavens
at times you drag me to earth
Oh give up with your echoes
and come up with clear moves
Let's fly to skies to bring that breeze of love
and let's breathe together to bless life to the soul of love
Oh let's be transparent and end the chaos
let's bring the springs and regain the tranquility
Come let's be true to one another and live together.

32. That innocence .

That innocence made an abode
deep in my heart
That lovely gaze of reverence
touched my soul
That heavenly bliss of his warmth
conjured my senses
That soulful rhythm of his voice
still beats in my core
The air I breathe in has the incense of his love
The spring is charming as that aura praises it
His each beat has musk of heavens
and presence is the repose of angels.

33. Years she stored.

Years she stored that love in her heart
tied with a devil she,
had given her soul to an angel
Met him never but roamed in his thoughts
praying to be free and fly with her angel,
she wanted to escape that beast who owned her
And one day she was relieved miraculously
her prayers when were answered
freed from that devil's arrestment when she flied away,
found him lost
lost he was in his sulkiness
tangled he was in his mess
And broken utterly she lied there
waiting for him to return
waiting for them to reunite.

9 798887 334714

Printed by Libri Plureos GmbH in Hamburg, Germany